PASSIONS FROM THE AGES

Alexander D. Ohemeng

Arlister Publication

Library Number:

ISBN: 978-9988-1-1699-6

Published by
Arlister Publication

Edited *by*

Agnes Vandyck

&

Cover Illustration *by*
Seyram Dzide

Dedication

*This work is dedicated
to these great women in my life;
My mother - Paulina
and
My wife - Agartha.*

CONTENTS

Acknowledgement

The useful role of an editor of Minerva Press; Andrew Grice on 27th April, 2000 must be recognised. It greatly influenced the resonant voice of these poems. Andrew Grice had only reviewed a part submission of *Passions from the Ages*. This was originally under the working title: *Whispers*.

The contribution from Andrew Grice in response to the first submission of an unedited version of this work was priceless. It gave hope and challenged the literary work to its present healthier state.

Mrs. Agnes Vandyck had a difficult role to play and her valuable part cannot simply be forgotten. At a personal cost of her own time, she edited these poems. Her contribution left the choice style much refined but originality still intact. Her input was immeasurable.

She brought to the work a professional background of an Educationist and Editor.

It must further be noted that apart from *'Fame and Wealth'* in this edited form, all other poems were completely inspired, and the sole work of the author.

'*Fame and Wealth*' was a poem chanced upon in a letter from my father to my mother, before his passing away into eternal glory.

Credit must also be given to my mother – Mrs. Paulina Amponsah-Arku for the enormous job she did; relentlessly encouraging the translation of these poetic inspirations into publication.

Mother's task was indeed a tough gig that was well executed in the phase of unaffordable offers even for publication. To a great extent, my mother was instrumental in my adventure of sharing this poetic food for thought with the general public.

The acknowledgement will not be complete without a gratitude to my wife.

The hint of some confusion from this woman of scholarship, after reading through the initial script was valuable. It simply led to the pursuit of simplicity above all other literary considerations.

Thanks to all others who have made this publication a reality.

Publication Note

Passions from the Ages is a promising work of poetry, intended for our reflection and pure pleasure.

The poet explores a range of themes and ideas, such as love, hope and fear, in a thoughtful manner. The poetic strings of preferred words were lightly structured.

It was the design of the poet to avoid the constraints of a strong rhyme and rhythm scheme in favour of a verse form. This had allowed him to develop his thoughts and feelings openly. You will find in some verses traces of desirable humour.

These selections of forty poems were part of other verses that had taken an average of forty days and forty nights to compose. However, it took fourteen more years to rid this particular work of unnecessary clutter, or call it the concealed weeds.

The arrangement of these verses had literary suffered many *hiccups* on the way to its publication, resulting in some deliberate reconstructions. Even in the mist of the changing surge of inspiration, the substance of this work of art remained unchanged.

It is hoped that these passions gathered from the ages will provoke a needed discussion for those of us concern about common social delusions and realities, ignored moral struggles, and some issues of relational utopia's that are worthy of poetic study.

The various concerns raised by this work are as much about our neighbours as they are about ourselves.

The
Liberated Soul

CAPTIVES

1

You may not wish to hear
That all will die;
But if I must die, before my death
It should never be to conscience
Nor beyond my *resurrection*
If I should be *dead*.

2

The demands and restraint
Of a conscience could be
A painful exercise;
But if the truth
About a Man redeemed be told
And a civilised people,
We be crowned,
Her yoke we choose to bear.

3

If conscience be confined
To a lone cell,
I will, a justified man
Crave to live even then with her;
A thousand more times,
Her captive;
As a man with a conscience.

AGAINST THE ODDS

1

To know
May bring no use but chaos
For the lack of wisdom
Or the absence of *faith.*

For without such wings to glide over
The impassible rift of existence,
A breeze could come our way
And against no odds, we may
Be swept away with no wings,
At least by faith
To rise.

2

The refuge in faith
Is the wisdom of its wings
Against the blustery winds of life.

All may need to mount, like eagles;
Soaring above much,
Perhaps, o'er life's nor'easters,
And against any odds ascend,
By godly faith to heights very much
Above many odds.

Love
or
Deceit?

LIKE A LADY

1

She looked like a lady for a man to seek.
But with some lens to perceive
she was revealed,
And with no doubts to the eye
As a lady clothed in deceit.

In a mist of shadows she had appeared,
like a lady, to desire.

2

She had the look- of a lady;
A wild flower,
Not so simply described,
from a different kingdom.
She was yet, but a real picture
of moulded perfection
With all the curves and turns of a woman,
well bred, you presume.

But then you learn, not always with age;
That the woman of apparent innocence
Could be the serpent that unfolds at dusk -
an angel of death.

3

She looks like a lady,
And with the grace of a cat
she moves with ease,
making her way into your thoughts.
In her eyes you could find
a shimmering gaze;
A flame that burns into a soul
with each smile she shared.

She could pass for a lady
With a beauty worth pursuing.
So in haste, we overlook the foundation
upon which she builds -
dear life.

4

She looks like a lady,
With the means to complete a Man.
So we daydream;
She could bring to an end
the thirst that came from youthful lust...
Because she looks like a lady,
to adore.

So the warning is often ignored
that she could be –
a mistress from hell's fire.

A BED OF ROSES

1

What have you to say
About thorns and roses?

For a groom or bride,
A bed of roses is a choice of bed
Where the fields you could explore,
The angels of God will dare not tread,
In this bed of roses.

2

For the groom or bride,
In a bed of roses
There're moments of great marvels,
And a great dawning,
When promises are made
On the first of most nights;
But there are thorns you may find,
In that bed, even of roses.

3

For the groom and the bride,
Until self or death do you part,
In that bed of roses
There are secrets to be learnt
By those who care to know.

It's for better or for worse;
A journey of a lifespan,
That you will cherish
Or you may wish to forget,
For there are various thorns
In that bed of roses.

4

For the groom and bride,
In a good bed of roses
There are scores of treaties
You are made to sign.
For a better bed of roses,
Or the best savor of your life
May be lost forever
In a rush to escape every thorn
In that bed of roses.

5

For the groom or bride
In some beds of roses:
You may discern the sacred things -
Even with thorns in that vine
How two could dine and dance
To the symphony of love
In a bed full of roses.

THE LOVE WEB

1

Profuse in a tender caress

Are flickering flames

Of many passions.

Suffused in the warmth of a touch

You may confess

There're countless charms;

Or else you may recount

The searing pains

And Unspeakable dishonor

In a web of a love assumed.

2

Found in each risked submission

To really love,

We may receive in part

A much yield in good returns,

Or a little more of some regrets

In love's depths of despair.

Profound in deified love -

Are the ever-lasting delights and tributes

Of a shared love,

Entangled in God's scheme of things;

Love is refined
        By an eternal fire.

WANTED

1

He was searching for a jewel
From among his friends;
A woman sublime was wanted
In his life for a wife
A woman, willing like him,
To adjust his life, for both their sake
To a different tuned life.

2

Wanted!
A wife for *Monsieur*?

Knowing this man so well,
It was a question to be asked.
But a wife was all he wanted,
He claimed;
To enlarge the sphere
Of a man's usefulness,
A companion is needed...
Not for a while, but all his live.

3

You could be wanted for a wife.
A beautiful face was not a must;
For the beauty of a soul,

Was what he sought.

About the burdens of imperfection

You must be willing, to bear your part

Of a hard day's work;

Pruning your soul and supporting each other

Till the end of your life.

4

I saw in *Monsieur*

A serenity of spirit.

For he has revealed

He searches for a wife, in all respect.

To start sincere, *Monsieur* admits;

A dowry of honour is all he has.

But he wants a good wife

And just one is all he needs.

So the best of fortunes,

I wish *Monsieur* –

He finds an excellent wife.

WHEN A MAN DECIDES

1

Oh man!
What an entity from God!
A paradox of sanity.
When a man from his hunger
Must choose to act,
Reason may well be buried,
And so much buried alive.

2

Oh man!
What trouble to man!
For when reason is called,
On duty to decide
What a victim the heart becomes.

3

Oh man!
What a contrast, to our image of God!
For when this heart of a man,
Is given the nod to make a choice
Daggers may be drawn
And for the rest
You can't be assured
Of what some man may decide.

Virtues
and
Vices

BETRAYED

1

For your work done well
You will be paid;
- With nothing of course.
Shocked! Mystified!!
They wished you well;
So well they refused to give,
Your due
In agreement for a service
Completed.

2

The injury is more severe
For each act of betrayal
From a service to a friend;
The cruelest of their vice
Is the extent some will go
To see you cash-strapped,
Or be *lynched* by debts
They will leave behind for you,
For a job well done.

3

Some friends are *generous*;
They will pay you less
shamelessly on purpose.

For the excellent work done
They offer their worse
A proverbial *wheel chair*
Of a greaseless kind,
When you are *crippled*
And made bankrupt
By their practice of betrayal
For a good work, thoroughly done,
But unpaid for.

DARK PLACES

1

In a closet within,
...Deep down within
Where the sunshine will not go
Is the darkest of all grounds,
Darker than the night
Where a *beast* resides
As thoughts untamed.

2

Where the light
Is hard to reach,
...The thoughts of darkness
May hide, and wait to pounce
Upon your sense of goodness
With such madness,
You never could believe
You had it all within.

3

In a closet within
...Deep down within us all
Where sufficient brightness
Of the light
Is not allowed to reach
Demons are left

On their own, unconquered,
Toying, with every whim
And every wish.

THE TEMPEST

1

For a twisted tale
And blinded pride,
We are taken by the tempest,
Fighting everyone, anyone
But for what?
A war,
For the furtherance of a man's folly
Over the *graveyards*
That will give no rest,
Even to the dead.

2

A little spark, is how it starts
Before our kith and kin
Are often dislodged
By the torrent of despair;
Our children and all
Are soon required to starve
But for what?
Their part of expense in a war
To obtain a *graveyard*
That gives no rest
To our dying people.

3

The blast of hot air
Could be the doing of another
Yet our silence
Shall spread the plague of death,
And the future
May well be gone in flames
And all for what?
But the sake of a *graveyard*
That can give no rest
To the living or the dead.

WHOSE FAULT?

1

The world and governments,
May be reeking very bad
But the mess is deeper than that:
Starting from our homes
Our training is worse;
With so many of our homes
A mere site
For sleepless nights
And yet you ask:
Whose fault?

2

Through the fraudulence indirectly condoned
By most of our kind
Many tokens of *thanks* are gathered.
Or for the pledge of one,
Some manage to extort the thanks
Before a task is simply began in earnest;
With a promise to be done, *almost well*
And yet you ask:
Whose fault?

3

A victim deplored, with irony
The corruption and the nuisance

None should suffer
Yet next,
We join the queue
To extract from another
A stolen pound of flesh
By hook or through the crook,
And yet we pose for debate
The subject of *whose Fault?*

Here and now;
Who must bear the blame?

HERITAGE

1

Let none be misled to forget
What led to our heritage
Of shame
Lest the grief of ignorance,
Or the verdict of a tyrant or a fool
Is again poured out for us
To be drunk by all.

For much suffering
Of centuries or decades passed
We cannot undo
But the hateful tides and the crimes
We deny they happened
Condemns generations unborn,
To a worse heritage.

2

Borrowed things,
Or our stolen wealth
We may wish were all recovered
By an offering for possible peace.
But the humans destroyed by enslavement;
We cannot restore,
Nor can we wish away this heritage
Of shame.

For we have stained with blood
Our earth,
And such things we cannot undo
But the wounds of our sentiments
And soul
Can better be healed;
By accepting repentance
And forgiving the experience,
We so harshly endured.

THE GRIM REAPER

1

The grim reaper
For all his sins, he loves to moan;
Because like a rat
Or even worse than one, he has been caught
In the way-ward ways
The wind to inherit
- The lot of a grim reaper.

2

A seed of misdeeds
The grim reapers do love to sow;
And when nothing more than weeds
Or a thorn-bush,
They will have for their harvest,
A wicked world
They blame the most
For all their woes, perhaps with tears
To express the state of their heart
- In a phony contriteness.

ECHOES

1

Freedom to the people!
Freedom for the people!
A soldier or not
They come to our aid, proclaiming
Our days of peace!
But soon our cities, our homes
And our people are shelled
Into forced submission
For the grievous of *sin*
They renounced the madness
Of any such adventurers.

2

Freedom to us for sure!
Freedom for sure!
For the echoes of our deliverers
Is made the loudest
By the stench of misdeeds.
Unable to believe
By those we elect for self-reliance.
For a little more say,
Before long they force into exile
The best from our lands
Because they spoke out too loud
And too much.

3

Freedom indeed for some!
Freedom for some!
For the hands that earns some bread
They will detach
With a threat from an axe
Of a terrible kind
Until you sink in fear
And you join their camp
Or you shrink with terror.

From a brutish rule,
We pray for salvation.

4

Freedom indeed for them!
Freedom for them!
Driven by the arm of greed
They loot our treasury,
And 'will' the rest, to a crony or two.
For all our grumble,
About their dogma of freedom

They will pass for law their lies
And for a *Bill of Right*;
An opportunity for a legalised theft.

THE MARKET VIPER

In the midst of a market crowd
Is a gathering of vipers.
Sometimes in the modest of wears;
Or in the richest attire
Of their coloured wraps
They are found,
At the market place,
With a catalogue of fabrications
for sale;
And almost for free,
They trade at such a price;
They could make a king,
Out of a monkey
And out of a shrewd,
A great fool.

THE UNHEEDED CRY

1

I hear above the roar
Of a man misinformed,
Or never informed;
The desperate sound
Of a woman's cry for help.

I hear a cry
For just a fair share
Of fairness.

2

I hear a terrible sound,
Not music badly played
But a feeble cry of dejection.

I hear a call
From a soul trampled upon.

3

I hear the sound of tears
From vessels so broken
I have felt them groan
For help never given.

I hear a cry

An unpleasant sound
Of the victims,
Of too many wrongs.

ARRIVE ALIVE

1

See how they speed!

On our streets and pavements;
Behind their wheels as though
From a sudden avalanche;
Or driven by the devil,
For more cash.

So you pay your fare
Then you wait in prayer;
To arrive home, alive.

2

See how they ride!

Obtaining a reckless writ
From the police, it seems;
They risk many lives
To rid themselves
Of the pestilence of poverty.

So you may well appeal
To arrive home, alive.

3

See how they drive!

In raving mockery of our hope
To see another blest day;
They run with no concern,
Except for their gain.

So in paying your fare in full
You might as well demand;
To *arrive home alive*
With each bone in place.

BOUND

1

Just once is how it starts,
Like many addictions:
To mask our fears
Or for a moment of pleasure:
Slowly, you are bound.
But as sure as death,
A shackle of a daily unrest
Awaits all who abuse
The potency of evil.

2

Just once!
May be one too many.
For once exposed
To a little dose of vice,
It might be all it takes
For a character defect,
With its heaps of sorrow;
For those who trifle
With the sacredness of life
You may be bound for hell,
Even here on earth.

FAME AND WEALTH

An edited epistle from my Father's Diary

1

Fame and wealth:
These are but lofty words
Banging on the sense and sensibility
Of mortal man.
For he could not help, but jot down
To the brethren today
Two perishable prizes;
Fame and wealth
For which men struggle
In ceaseless combat, cruel
Yet bringing no absolute-satisfaction.

2

Fame and wealth:
They are but toys
That pleases for a time
Then becomes too wearisome.
But conquering self is a battle
In which victory bestows a deeper content;
A larger happiness,
And a more perfect peace
That neither poverty nor sickness,
Nor the gravest misfortune,

Can destroy;
Or abate the ardour of the warrior
Who is absorbed in a crusade
Against his own worse passions.

3

Fame and wealth:
They so easily give birth to egotism
A common vice of our age
And a maxim of the ever present;
Each man a lover of self
And not of his neighbour,
Not even his friends.
In such a state of things
When personal interest
Is the only gain desired,
We cannot look for honesty
In either politics, or commerce;
Or even in art and religion -
When all the finer sentiments
And nobler instincts of men are made
Subject to mammon-worship.
Are we so blind to think it conveys
The divine will, to this age?
Nothing but evil will accrue
From such a system.

To those who have prophetic eyes

See through the veil of events
And perceive even now
In the nearing distances: the end.

*Changing
Tides*

WINDS OF CHANGE

1

The passing winds of time
The dried leaves announce
And if the adage
About time be fact,
There comes a time,
A time for all things.

.

2

There are blissful times
When you may wine and dance
But if the adage
About life be true,
There are those times, the sad times
When you never could dance.
But the time may come, and much too soon
To let go so much, sometimes too much.
Or you must resolve
Holding on, firmly on;
Before time is forever lost
In the winds of change.

3

There are certain times
The ageing bones foretell

The coming winds of change
When you give no ears;
Or you offer them both
For what the wise must say; or else
Be damned by the winds of change.
But if the adage
About knowing be accurate
There comes a time unknown
When the answers to what's important
Is left to the winds of change.

TIME WILL TELL

1

Time will tell,
But what stories about you?

There are periods
We may nag or frown at time
Or we align with time;
The essence of such times
The future will confirm.

2

Time will tell
But what tales about you?

For all the time you need
Some you find and some you don't.
A real puzzle is the nature of time
For each one of us to solve
That relation of a sequence;
To either fail or succeed with time,
The present will define.

QUEEN OF THE NIGHT

1

What a nerve she has! So calm
Beside the Lord of Day who is so stern.
Behind the brightness of the astral
She is ever so hard to see at day.
In the hours of darkness
She may reign over much;
As a lamp of a lustrous grey.
For she lies in wait, ever so quiet
For the night to be Queen.

2

Beyond our skies, among the stars,
Beneath the heavens
Of scattered goodness,
The mortal nights she may touch;
Some to be changed, others to be stirred
By this Queen, of the night.

THE KNIGHT

1

He was a knight so strange:
A fearless cloud in frosty white.
The gloomy skies so blue it was black;
He traversed
With the ease of an ancient champion,
Taunting a colossal foe
In the mist of lightning bolts...
He defied that heavy rain
Mounted on a dancing wild horse.

2

In a shade of a coloured armor:
He rode by in victory,
A drifting cloud,
On a strangest of mare with a tapering horn,
But he rode in a thundering chaos
Across the changing skies of day...
And among the stars at night
He was still a Knight to remember.

GREY

1

Much questions about grey;
It must be more
than being too old and grey
When the vigour of youth
May well be sapped,
And tissues are patched
Or they cannot be mended.

It must be more.

2

About the era of being grey;
It must be more
Than a time for wrinkles
And the fewer to be seen
A guarantee of limited frustrations
For a soul so old and grey.
The trace of grey
Could be wisdom personified.

But it must be more.

PROSPECTS

1

He was grey and frail
With a grip on a stick for walking,
He stopped and stooped for a while,
And he stares at the haste of those around.
His words were unspoken by mouth
For he shook his head
With the look in his eyes
His thoughts were revealed;

"Some may learn
About the cost of a genuine toil,
In many years to come.
The price might be too long in paying,
And our life too short,
Enjoying the yields we may have ploughed".

Such are the prospects of many an ordinary Man.

2

He was gray and bent
With his stick to help
He stood low for a little while,
Signing with relief,
He suddenly stood up so tall,
And hopeful

With a radiance in his outlook
He walked away content.
For he seems to have toiled so well
And he had mined the profits of hard work;
For his off-spring - a better chance
To build for themselves - a better life.

Such are the prospects of many a Man of vision.

Living Memories

THE HERALD

1

Who deserves the name;
The oppressor's nightmare?
He who comes with a cask of ink,
Writing and divulging, to whom he must
The infamy of abused rights.

So all arise, to hail this herald
Who inscribes his every word
For the sake of those forsaken.

2

Who deserves the praise;
The devil's regret?
It could be one
Who may tend to print,
Your woes for sale;
But with the greatest of tools,
From the trade he plies,
He does unearth, the truth we need
With the prudence demanded
To break the unbroken shackles
Of deceit.

So all arise and hail
Every one of those heralds

Who have earned this name.

3

Who deserves the honours
Of Human remembrance?
He whose pen is sharper
Than a sword
But he carves with care,
The liberty of Man;
With the sense to guide,
He searches his soul and gives his best;
For more than bills to defray,
Scandals to disclose or people to ridicule.
For he dares to keep alive
Freedom and justice,
Writing, each word,
Sometimes, to our grief...

Let us all arise and hail
The endangered heralds
Who lives their days today,
So others can live.

THE SCAVENGER

1

There he goes again,
the *Man-Scavenger*
With emptied cans
and long-forgotten wares;
To up-lift the face of art
and imaginations
to stretch.

2

He roams the earth
from dawn till tired
the likes of scraps;
The gold abandoned
The *Man-Scavenger* finds
to refine into a breath of art
so grand
and so greatly, divine.

THE FIRM

1

A reputable firm
Does require someone
For immediate appointment:
'Whom you know',
Could be your fortune for employment;
But as good as taken
If you, by proof can *stand*,
On both your legs
Alone for *the firm*.

2

A vacant post,
Is available for you.
They want someone
For a night watchman;
But with your sight a little impaired,
It could be bad for you;
For the bother of barricades
Will be left in your way.

3

You need this job?
With a hearing defect
To the ravings of man or boss
The reaction could often be worse;

He may despise your lot.

Could you endure on this job?

4

Are you looking for a job?
For a convict who is even reformed
Your chances are slim,
Or none at all.
For they may be *'banished'*
From the list of unemployed;
Or they may accept,
That you are hired, if you will toil
Only for breadcrumbs.

5

Employed by *The firm*?
The proper smile or the right bite
Is surely a plus
For immediate promotion,
But your wrong barks
Could send you out
With immediate effect.

Who wants this job?

6

You really want this job?

A curious mind is not so bad,
But you will be troubled, when you are in.
So a strong jaw they will approve
For the obvious intent.

You still want this job?

7

Accepted by *the firm*?
You, could soon be fired
All for a broken limb,
And the excuse will be simple;
It's bad for business
But if you, with half a limb
Can dance to the tune of *The firm*,
Your story could be different.

8

Who will have this job
With no one to help?
The post could be yours.
But for you,
Our newest of graduates
The firm maintains,
They want someone
With experienced years of five
Or you must have spent

Just one of your years
Preferably, in space.

Can you get this job?

FORGOTTEN

1

To those we all forgot
And to those never named
In the house of honours
We say: *Merci to you,*
Who were submerged in service:
For you rose and set like the sun,
Perhaps, more radiant even than the sun.

2

Merci to them who diligently served:
A living proof
For intricate Man
And a revered beacon
For ordinary Man.

They often were mortals,
But were greater than self;
For they were heroes and heroines
Before the world could accept
They've worked, deserving our thanks.

3

Merci to them, who majestically rose:
And for each cost of being free,
They gave the dearest of possessions -

Their lives.

Merci to you; our bravest of hearts
Who in dying
Gave power to our dreams so long deferred

By the turmoil of our mentality.

4

To those too soon forgotten
We say to you; *Merci beaucoup*
For what you are worth.

The irony of our errors
Are the unnumbered stars of hope
We never knew;
The little man and woman
And their wits, or feats of greatness
We only might admit,
When they are dead and gone.

We say to these - *Merci beaucoup.*

MAN-GO-STAND

1

What kind of a man is he
Whose old and broken shoulders
Could not hold too well
And yet all that is left for *self*
He gives away
To others on their way to the grave
Like himself
With just one remark to all
Man-go-stand?

What manner of a man is he
Who will not be silenced
That *Man-go-stand*
Though living a life so grim?

2

Who really is he
Misconstrued for a man so weak
Being so meek.
Ridden to a bed he could not leave,
And in the cold grips of death
He will still not doubt
That *Man-go-stand*.?

What man is he,

Who could still be heard
From beyond the grave
That *Man -go- stand?*

OUR MEN IN BROWN

1

Gone are the noble old days
Of our men in brown.
Around they came, those days
In a baggy shorts of brown,
A size for two, gathered at the knee.
They appeared for work;
In a shirt of creaseless brown,
Wearing a helmet of white
And a pair of white socks, some wore to match
A black boot or shoe,
With a ladle in their bag or belt
- The water pots to stir for worms.

Gone, it seems
Are the useful old days
Of our men in brown.

2

I am not too sure – Why,
But Town-Council Man
We called the men in brown.
A valued force, they used to be
Despite our constant disputes with them.
Though they had our health in mind,
They still earned but a few friends

When a hefty fine for negligence
We are made to settle.

Gone, it seems
Are the good old days
Of our men in brown.

3
The cooking places
Must be freed from dirt and flies.
Your friend or not,
The waste should be out,
And your home be kept
Safe from germs
And mosquitoes that we breed;
Or the weight of bye-laws,
Would be thrown at you
By the sanitary inspectors.

Gone, it seems
Are the clean old days -
With our men in brown.

MY HOME

1

In my home -
A little stretch across the Fante shores
Is a coastal town - Beyond *'The Birds Rock'*
Given its name, by a peculiar stone,
Some insist; a titular deity
Upon whose summit within the sea
The sea gulls do sit in court
And to have their sport.
But here in my home stands Fort William
From whence had floated in the past
The Union Jack and *polished sticks*
That spat fire upon those not welcome
To the king's court.

2

In my home -
A distance or more along our shores
From whence the sea sand is lined with gold,
Rest the remains of my poor country folks.
But here in my mother's home;
- Beyond *'The Bird's Rock'*
Our native poets had spoken of a mystery;
For we fetched our water with baskets,
Conveyed with thorns to our homes.

In my home -

Along our coast - Beyond *'The Birds Rock'*

The English and others came to trade

Rattling, in different tongues

But across my home, they seized by force,

People like goods.

From within and behind the walls of Fort William

My people were sold for a pot of rum

By family or a foe

Their lives were chained

Until they were freed, often by death,

Away from home.

Innocent
Rascals

ALUTA CONTINUA

1

Aluta continua
There is a tussle of two worlds;
Between the old and young in years
Each one of them
With a singular claim:
They've come to discern
Definitely better.

So Aluta continua
This struggle may not end
Until both are willing to gain
From what the other may have learnt.

2

Aluta continua
From experience of a long life
The old demand respect,
But the young protest to be heard,
If deserved.

So Aluta continua
This struggle goes on
Until we all can agree
That both could be right
And courtesy ought to prevail.

3

Aluta continua
Each one asserts it is time to lead,
Or they were born to lead;
With none prepared to fellow,
And none to resign
To the ways of the other.

So Aluta continuer
This struggle may never end
Until common sense will yield
To absolute truth.

BEWARE

1

The laws of a Dad
Often they warn; Beware of rascals
Beware of dogs, my child beware.

A mother is normally nice.
She extends a hand of welcome
To those who are friends.
Yet, her decrees are pronounced;
All hands, every hand
Must be off my child!

She may turn, later to her child
And without a smile, she warns:
Beware my love, beware of dogs -
So many in sheep's clothing!

2

In the reign of King Dad
Or is it our Mums?
You are warned;
'Be aware of this, and beware of that.
Beware of him, or her or them.
Yes my dear, beware of wolves -
For so many are nicely clothed!'

3

Be wary of the stray fox
For there are so many on the loose
And so we are warned to beware.

But for a never ending tune
To be careful of many things
Some may ask, but why?

Why, can we not but be left alone
To live our lives, our own way?
Why you cannot do as you please
For Sweet Mum or Dear Dad
To pay for it all?

And you wonder why?

4

With a bad grade or worse,
The General called Mum may fuss,
But beware, King Dad may explode
At the sight of rebellion
Or an alliance into one.

And yet you ask why?
Why their wisdom must not be scorned?
Take heed and beware;
For there are strangely clothed dogs.

THE NOBLE ONES

1

They make an entrance
From the sheltered walls
Of a mother's womb;
Ready or not
The *noble* ones, usually arrive
With screams and clenched fist.
They want your best
From all your rest.

2

The *noble* ones may arrive
Amidst the chaos to a new world;
Your laundry will not,
In the least be safe from all the stains.
As they pitch or spit their meals
All at you.

3

Out of a cradle?
The *noble* ones may get to work
On all that strike their fancy;
They scatter your belongings,
And flood your home
And yet they want an answer
To why grown-ups,

Are ever so hard to live with.

4

The *noble* ones could make our neighbors
Or the family pet, ill at ease.
They leave us spent
But to our surprise
We want them back
To love them more
When it's time for them
To live our homes.

Turning Points

BEYOND OUR MEANS

1

It is often our grief
Life hurts so bad, the budget pill
Cannot be swallowed.
Eagerly awaiting pay-day,
We find the times too hard
We cannot afford to subsist.
Some are ever wont to say:
It's so little, the wage we earn
And yet so much
Beyond our means,
From the world to covet;
It is hard to live.

2

No one should ask of us
That we live on bare bones;
But if in spite of the limited store,
The wise could accept
To live within their means;
Then we might,
With so little,
In time afford the choice
To live content,
And better than a king.

3

Our needs

Or just our wants?

A distinction must be made,

And those acts of waste

Must be well addressed

To avoid *the pathos of a hard life:*

Living on needless credit.

CLUTTER

1

If anyone was ever set
To give the best
He was sure
He had a plot and the words
For a master piece.

But then he could taste, in the mouth
The sourness of a cluttered speech.

2

If anyone understood for sure
What letters from the soul
To be expressed,
He knew of those words
Which are bound to explain themselves
For the skeptics to agree;
The thoughts cohered in rhythm
To a Bonwire loom.

But then he could not dispel, from the mind
The likely clutter in his words.

3

If a writer was never confused

It was the subject he chose,
He was certain of the required structure
For it was narrative here,
And descriptive there
A little subjective now and then
But for what he had on substance,
The critics may agree;
It was most objective, with no litter of tenses.

Yet he could sense on his part
A clutter of doubt, there in his heart.

FROM THE DEEP

1

On the sea of fate, I found a man adrift.
He was so wet by tears and so deep in prayer,
He implored the Lord:
'To the rescue my God, redeem my life,
For the light grows dim,
My feet grow cold,
And my soul is undone.'

2

Adrift, on the waves of fate I saw a man
He was soft-spoken, and in tears,
He spoke in a tongue
So piercing from the deep;
'Remember, my God, remember...
Restore my hope, for I see no wind
To carry me ashore.'

AWAKE AND LIVE

1

Why, O my soul
Are thou perturbed
Beyond concern?

Why, O my soul
Be so afraid over yet
The unknown tomorrow;
Neglecting the hopes thou have,
Today?

Awake O my soul and believe.

2

Awake, O my soul!
And wallow not in the mud
Of yester years;
Drowning thyself
In such regrets
For wasted years,
And losing sleep
Over the nameless care
Of the coming days.

Awake O my soul and be watchful.

3

Awake O my soul!

For the past is gone,

But the future by *grace* can be changed

And by works be established tomorrow.

But all must be well started today.

Awake then O my soul and live, even now.

DREAMS

1

Sad to see and be said,
That a dream was wrecked.
Like a weathering rock,
Before my eyes.
It was shattered into dust,
Left to the winds
And I - *a broken spirit.*

2

Before the sun will rise
What becomes of any man
With no dream,
Or a mangled dream?

I was but a stranded man
On a desert of illusions,
With clouded visions;
I was lost,
Left behind, I presumed
By the *dream maker.*

I was but a man,
In a desert storm
With no assurance of hope

Before my sight was fully restored.

3

On a desert or not,
Soon you will learn
A Man must dream or else he dies.
But I intend to live my life to the full;
Reaching up, for impossible skies
That I could hold.

The looming cost will best be paid
If I will dream awake, a better dream,
A never-ending dream,
Even before the dawn will break
And the sun will rise.
I will dream.

Reader's Note